Spelling Made Easy

Key Stage 2

AGES 8–9

Author Huw Thomas

Certificate

Congratulations to

....
(write your name here)

for successfully finishing this book.

GOOD JOB!

You're a star.

Date

....

DK | Penguin Random House

DK London
Editors Elizabeth Blakemore, Jolyon Goddard
Managing Editor Christine Stroyan
Managing Art Editor Anna Hall
Senior Production Editor Andy Hilliard
Senior Production Controller Jude Crozier
Jacket Design Development Manager Sophia MTT
Publisher Andrew Macintyre
Associate Publishing Director Liz Wheeler
Art Director Karen Self
Publishing Director Jonathan Metcalf

DK Delhi
Senior Editor Rupa Rao
Senior Art Editor Stuti Tiwari Bhatia
Editor Rohini Deb
Art Editor Dheeraj Arora
Assistant Art Editor Kanika Kalra
Managing Editors Soma B. Chowdhury, Kingshuk Ghoshal
Managing Art Editor Govind Mittal
DTP Designers Anita Yadav, Rakesh Kumar, Harish Aggarwal
Senior Jacket Designer Suhita Dharamjit
Jackets Editorial Coordinator Priyanka Sharma

This edition published in 2020
First published in Great Britain in 2016 by
Dorling Kindersley Limited
DK, One Embassy Gardens, 8 Viaduct Gardens, London, SW11 7BW

The authorised representative in the EEA is
Dorling Kindersley Verlag GmbH. Arnulfstr. 124,
80636 Munich, Germany

20 19 18 17 16
016–196494–May/2020

A CIP catalogue record for this book is available from the British Library.
ISBN 978-1-4093-4947-1

Printed and bound in China

www.dk.com

MIX
Paper | Supporting responsible forestry
FSC™ C018179

This book was made with Forest Stewardship Council™ certified paper – one small step in DK's commitment to a sustainable future.
Learn more at www.dk.com/uk/information/sustainability

Contents

This chart lists all of the topics in the book. When you complete each page, colour in a star in the correct box. When you've finished the book, sign and date the certificate.

Alphabetical order

FACTS

Knowing **alphabetical order** is essential for finding words in a dictionary, entries in an index and books on library shelves.

Look at the words in each cloud. Sort the words into alphabetical order. Circle the first word, then draw an arrow from the first word to the second, the second to the third and so on. One has been done for you.

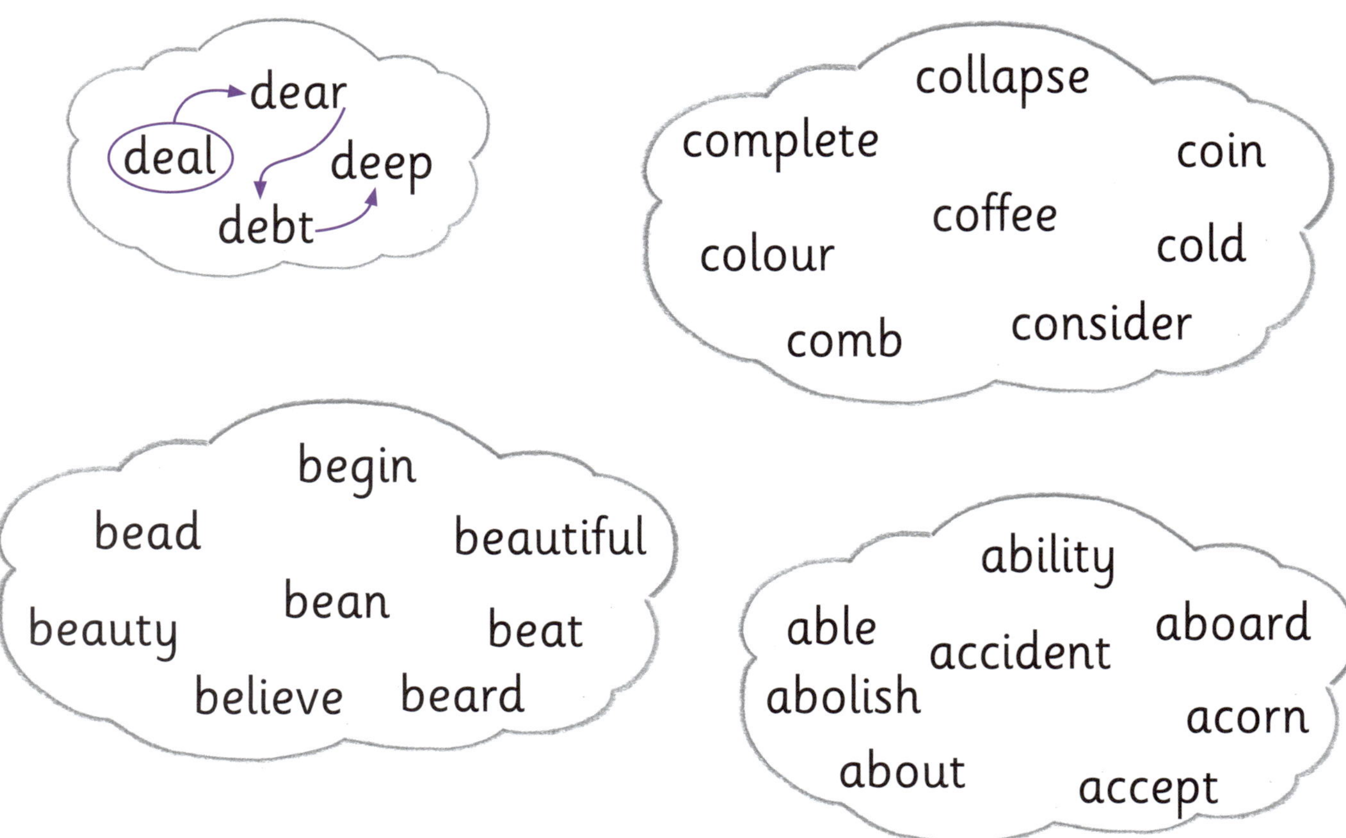

Now list all the words in the clouds above in alphabetical order.
For example: the words in the **d** cloud would be listed as: deal, dear, debt, deep.

a	b	c ....
a	b	c ....
a	b	c ....
a	b	c ....
a	b	c ....
a	b	c ....
a	b	c ....
a	b	c ....

Root words

A **root word** is a word to which groups of letters may be added to make other words.

Find the words that have the same root word and write them under the correct group heading below.

happily	written	friendly	liked	writes	happiest
likeness	friends	likes	happiness	joyful	befriend
unhappy	terrible	enjoyable	unlikely	terrorise	unfriendly
writer	enjoyment	writing	terrify	enjoying	terrific

joy	like	write
....	....	....
....	....	....
....	....	....
....	....	....

happy	friend	terror
....	....	....
....	....	....
....	....	....
....	....	....

Real words

FACTS

Words are spelled by joining letter sounds together. Some words are real, such as **light**, and other words are not real, such as **dight**.

Complete this chart by joining the starter sounds to the end sounds. Circle all the real words. One has been done for you.

Starter sounds	End sounds			
	ight	**own**	**ump**	**ear**
br	bright			
cl				
fr				
d				
j				
l				
n				
p				
sl				
t				

Homophones

Homophones are words that sound the same but have different spellings and meanings. For example:

hole and whole | wait and weight

Look at the homophone pairs in the balloons. Complete these sentences using these words.

We played with .... friends.

We played outside for an ....

We can .... the beach.

I played in the ....

Write four sentences using the homophones in the balloons below.

....

....

....

....

....

....

Can you think of some more homophone pairs?

....

....

Common homophones

FACTS

The word **homophone** comes from the Greek words for **same** and **sound**.

Here are three pairs of common homophones.

Homophones	Meanings	Examples
their	shows something is owned	Their shoes belonged to them.
there	points to a place	The shop is over there.
to	towards a place or person	Give the bag to him.
too	also or as well	I went shopping and Claire came, too.
see	to look at something	I can see you.
sea	a vast amount of salt water	The boat sails on the sea.

Write six sentences using the homophones above.

....

....

....

....

....

....

Spellings to learn

our hour rain reign new knew heard herd to too

Rhyming words

FACTS

Words with the same endings often **rhyme**, as in **right** and **fight**.

Read the words in the book below. Find the seven pairs of rhyming words and write them on the lines. Time yourself. How long does it take you to match and write all the rhyming pairs?

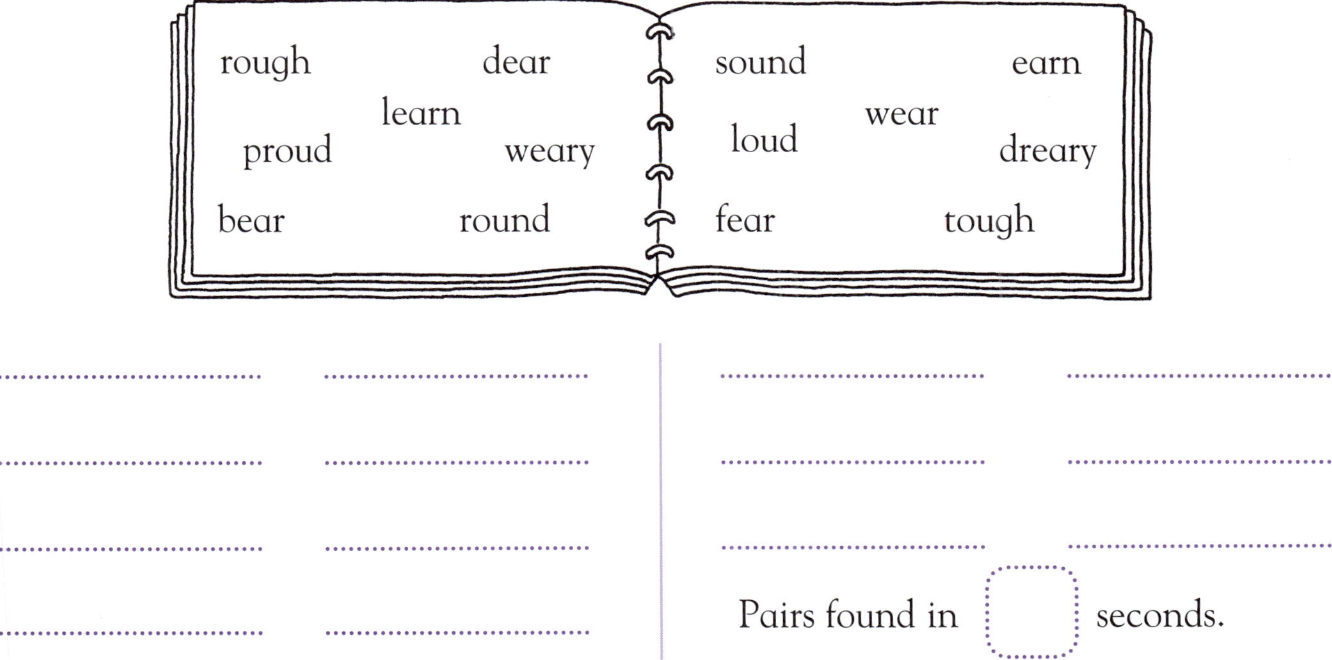

Pairs found in .... seconds.

Now find seven groups of three rhyming words on this list. Time yourself.

sight applause ice
should nice pause
thigh your
high pour would
bright eight
cause sigh mice
freight weight
four light could

Groups found in .... seconds.

Verb endings

FACTS

A **verb** is a doing, or action, word. It tells us what happens in a sentence. It can have different endings.

The endings tell us if the action happened in the **past** (for example: **she played**) or if the action happens in the **present** (for example: **she plays** or **she is playing**).

Make three new words from each root verb by adding the different endings. One has been done for you.

Root verbs	Add **s**	Add **ed**	Add **ing**
shout	shouts	shouted	shouting
look			
climb			
kick			
learn			
cook			
wait			
laugh			
clean			

Rules about verb endings

FACTS

When adding **ed** or **ing** to **root verbs**, there are rules to remember.

For most root verbs, just add **ed** or **ing**. For example: **cook**, **cooked** and **cooking**.

For root verbs ending with a **short vowel** and a **consonant**, such as **op**, **ab**, **at** or **it**, double the last letter and then add **ed** or **ing**. For example: **stop**, **stopped** and **stopping**.

Now use these rules to add **ed** and **ing** to each of the root verbs below.

Root verbs	Add **ed**	Add **ing**
drop	....	....
call	....	....
fit	....	....
grab	....	....
jump	....	....
hop	....	....
trap	....	....
slip	....	....
play	....	....

More rules about verb endings

FACTS

Verbs can be changed by adding **ed** and **ing**. When verbs that end in **y** or **e** are changed, there are a couple of rules to remember.

For a **root verb** ending in **e**, drop the **e** before adding the ending.

For a root verb ending in a **consonant** and **y**, change the **y** to **i** before adding **ed**, but keep the **y** before adding **ing**.

Add **ed** and **ing** to each of the root verbs below. One has been done for you.

Root verbs	Add **ed**	Add **ing**
hate	hated	hating
change	....	....
wave	....	....
skate	....	....
fade	....	....
move	....	....

Add **ed** and **ing** to each of the root verbs below. One has been done for you.

Root verbs	Add **ed**	Add **ing**
marry	married	marrying
try	....	....
cry	....	....
deny	....	....
rely	....	....
carry	....	....

More rules about verb endings

FACTS

Verbs can be changed by adding **s** or **es**, but there are some rules to remember.

For most verbs, just add **s**. For example: **I add** and **she adds**.

For a verb ending in a **consonant** and **y**, change the **y** to **i** and then add **es**. For example: **I worry** and **she worries**.

For a verb ending in a soft sound, such as **ss**, **sh**, **ch** and **x**, add **es**. For example: **I fix** and **she fixes**.

Use the rules above to change the following root verbs.

I look →	She	....
I find →	He	....
I play →	Liam	....
I envy →	She	....
I help →	He	....
I pass →	Jo	....
I run →	He	....
I rush →	She	....
I want →	He	....
I wish →	Carla	....
I catch →	It	....
I cry →	He	....
I make →	It	....
I try →	She	....
I change →	It	....
I carry →	Carol	....
I push →	He	....
I fall →	She	....

Roots and verbs

FACTS

Remember: a **verb** is a doing, or action, word.

Read the following verbs and find groups of three words with the same root verb. One has been done for you.
Hint: look for three verbs that start with the same letters.

make writing making made
keeping taking take
kept see catch know
wrote keep took
knew write seeing saw
caught knowing catching

....
....
....

....
....
....

....
....
....

take
took
taking

....
....
....

....
....
....

....
....
....

Irregular verbs

FACTS

Not all verbs follow regular verb rules. For example: the past form of **run** is not **runned** but **ran**. We call these **irregular verbs**.

Sort the irregular verbs in the verb box into their present and past forms. One has been done for you.

give	can	found	told	see	take	had	am	knew	make	took	went
go	eat	know	tell	ate	made	could	was	saw	gave	have	find

Present	Past
see	saw
....	....
....	....
....	....
....	....
....	....
....	....
....	....
....	....
....	....
....	....
....	....

Making verbs

FACTS

Some **nouns** and **adjectives** can be made into **verbs** by adding **suffixes**. A suffix is a group of letters that can be added to the end of a **root word** to change its meaning.

For example: **apology** (noun) + **ise** = **apologise**
deep (adjective) + **en** = **deepen**

Remember: a noun is a word that names something;
an adjective is a word that describes a noun.

Draw a line to match each of the verbs to a noun or an adjective.

Nouns	Verbs	Adjectives
criticism	possess	special
reality	decorate	real
decoration	realise	sad
possession	specialise	pure
identity	loosen	loose
education	criticise	hard
	sadden	
	identify	
	educate	
	harden	
	purify	

The prefix "al"

FACTS

A **prefix** is a group of letters that can be added to the beginning of a root word to change its meaning. The prefix **al** means **all**.

Add the prefix **al** to each of these root words and then write sentences in the speech bubbles using the new words.

al words

__so	__ways	__most
__though	__one	__ready

Adding prefixes

FACTS

Remember: a **prefix** changes the meaning of a root word.

Each of the words below has a prefix: **ad**, **al**, **af** or **a**. Write each word in its correct prefix group.

advice	adjective	asleep	already	also	ahead	alike	affect
almost	away	affirm	always	affix	adverb	admire	afflict

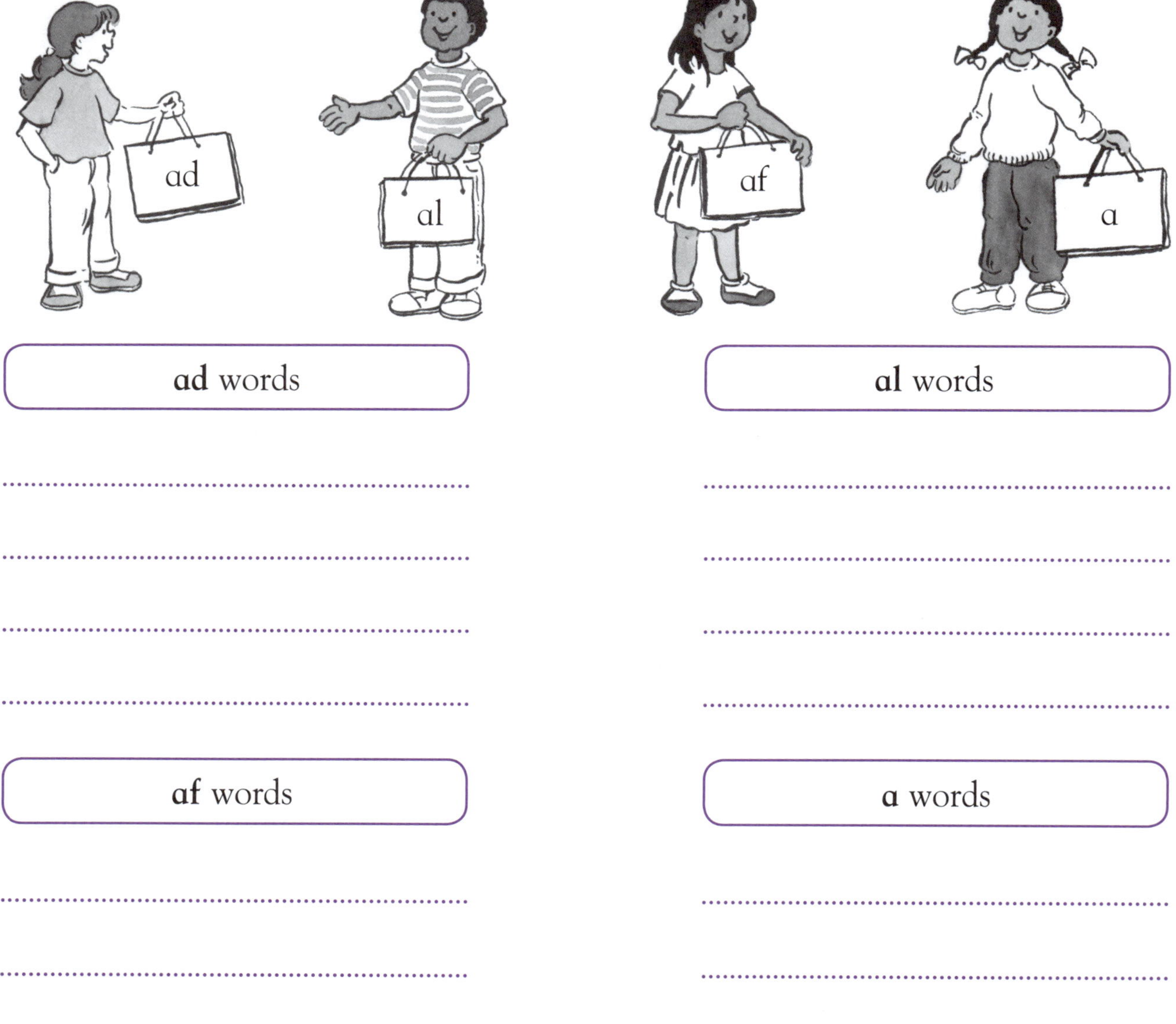

ad words

....

....

....

....

al words

....

....

....

....

af words

....

....

....

....

a words

....

....

....

....

Look in a dictionary for two more words in each prefix group. Add them to the correct list. Now learn the spellings of the words in each group.

Word bluff ★

FACTS

The suffixes **ship, hood, ness** and **ment** are called **state suffixes**. They are used to change root words into new words that describe the state of being something.

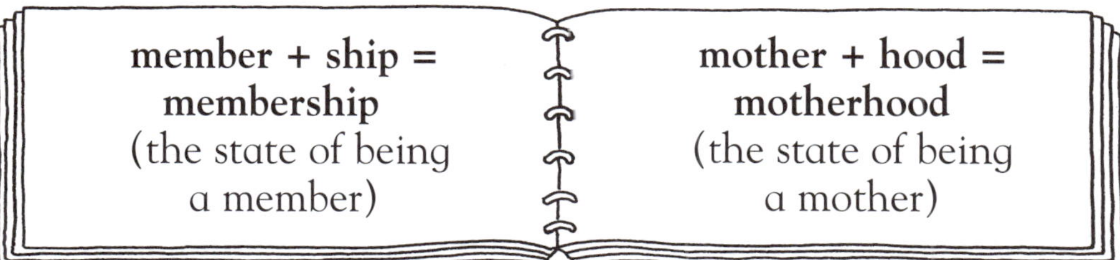

Each box below contains a definition and two words. One of the two words is correct and the other is made up. Circle the correct word.

the state of being a knight knightship knighthood	the state of being a friend friendhood friendship
the state of being a champion championship championhood	the state of being punished punishment punishship
the state of enjoying something enjoyness enjoyment	the state of being dark darkness darkment
the state of owning something ownerment ownership	the state of being amused amusement amusehood
the state of being astonished astonishment astonishhood	the state of being ill illness illship
the state of being fit fitness fitment	the state of being a child childhood childship

The "ight" and "tion" endings

FACTS

Two common word endings are **ight** and **tion**.

How many words can you make by joining the endings **ight** or **tion** to each of the beginnings below? List the words in the numbered spaces. Can you fill all the spaces?

Beginnings	
br	**sta**
ac	**ton**
decora	**men**
na	**n**
stra	**rela**
fr	**fre**
del	**posi**

1 ....

2 ....

3 ....

4 ....

5 ....

6 ....

7 ....

8 ....

9 ....

10 ....

11 ....

12 ....

13 ....

14 ....

I scored [ ] points.

Root roads ★

Remember: there is only one **l** in the suffix **ful**.

Start at a root word (on the left) and drive to a suffix (on the right) that will make a new word. Write the new word on a dotted line.

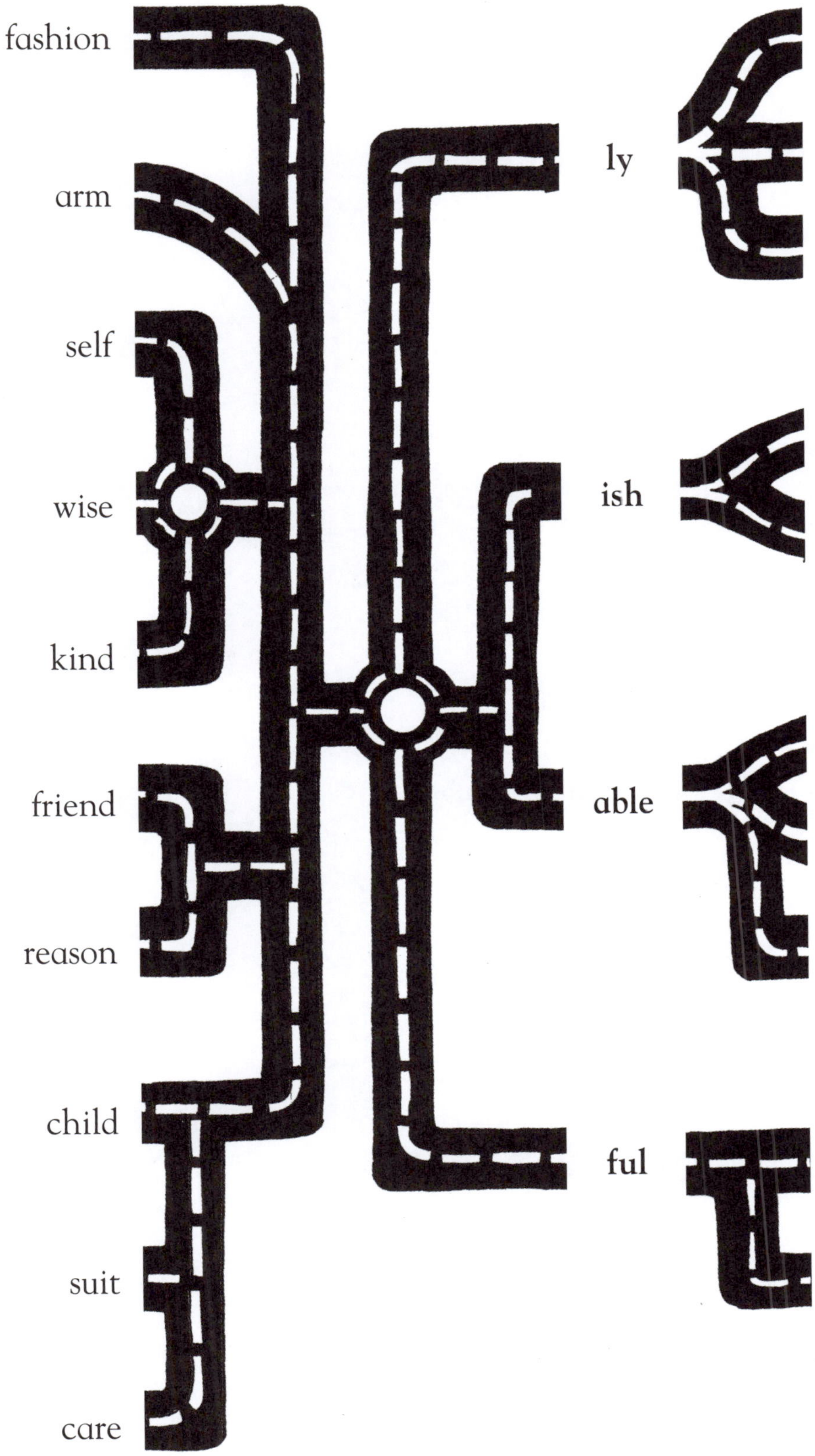
fashion
arm
self
wise
kind
friend
reason
child
suit
care
ly
ish
able
ful

★ Suffix maze

FACTS

Remember: the final **e** in some words is dropped before the suffix **ive** is added, as in **expense** + **ive** = **expensive**.

On the maze, draw a line joining each root word on the left to a suffix on the right to make one of the words in the box below.

helpful	expensive	gladly
artist	careful	active

Spellings to learn

recent action tonight lovely careful friendly

FACTS

Some suffixes sound similar, such as **ible** and **able**; **tion** and **sion**.

The suffix **able** usually follows a root word that makes sense on its own. For example: **agree** makes sense on its own.

The suffix **ible** usually follows a root that is not an actual word. For example: if you take the **ible** from **horrible**, it leaves **horr**.

Complete the following words using **ible** or **able**. Use a dictionary to check your answers.

terr..........................	comfort......................
reason......................	imposs......................
sens..........................	remark......................
suit..........................	laugh........................
vis............................	horr..........................
poss..........................	agree........................

Complete the following words using **tion** or **sion**. Use a dictionary to check your answers.

divi..........................	televi........................
explo........................	competi.....................
informa....................	protec.......................
inven........................	inva..........................
revi..........................	na............................
ten...........................	ac............................
vi............................	publica.....................

 Making plurals

FACTS

For **singular nouns** that end in **f**, **ff** or **fe**, there are three rules to remember when making them **plural**.

If the word ends in a single **f**, you usually change **f** to **v** and add **es**.

For example:

scarf

scarves

If the word ends in **fe**, change **fe** to **ves**.

For example:

wife

wives

If the word ends in **ff**, just add **s**.

For example:

cuff

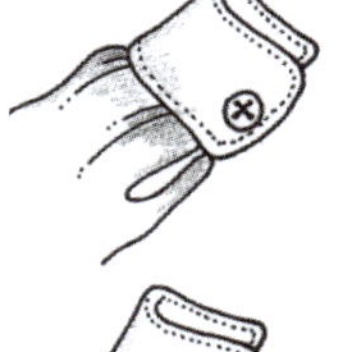

cuffs

Write the plurals for these singular nouns.

 one leaf → many ....  

 one thief → many ....  

 one cliff → many .... 

 one loaf → many .... 

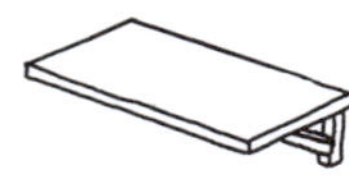 one shelf → many .... 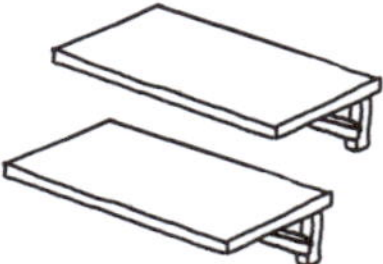

 one sniff → many .... 

Double consonants 

FACTS

Word games and puzzles are great ways to learn spellings.

Each of the clues below is for a word with double consonants, such as lesson. Solve the clues and then fill in the puzzles. Some letters are given to help you.

Across

1 Tied together with rope

2 Untidy or dirty

3 Bread and ....

4 Baby cat

5 Foolish or lacking sense

6 You sense this with your nose

		1 k						d
	2 m				y			
3 b					r			
4 k					n			
5 s				y				
6 s				l				

Can you see two more words with double consonants in these puzzles? Draw a line around these words.

						1 s				y
	2 p				o					
					3 h				o	
				4 s					r	
			5 s							g
		6 r					t			
	7 s							g		
8 r						g				

Across

1 Apologetic

2 You sleep with your head on it

3 An animal that loves mud

4 Season after spring

5 Losing weight

6 Small animal with long ears

7 Buying things

8 Faster than walking

Strings and sounds

FACTS

Some **letter strings** make different sounds when they are used in different words. For example: the letters **oo** sound different in b**oo**k and h**oo**t.

Look at the words in the word box. Write the words with the same letter strings in the correct letter string list.

tool	screw	foot	blood	mission	chemist
loose	work	chop	bench	ascend	session
worn	waste	swam	punch	lesson	scrape
miss	was	swan	worth	sword	science

ch	**oo**	**sc**
....	....	....
....	....	....
....	....	....
....	....	....

wa	**ss**	**wor**
....	....	....
....	....	....
....	....	....
....	....	....

Spellings to learn

daring swimming playful beautiful reasonable television

It's and its

FACTS

It's (with an **apostrophe**) is a shortened form of **it is**. The apostrophe marks the place where one or more letters have been taken out. In **it's**, the apostrophe marks the place of the missing **i**.

Its (without an apostrophe) is a **possessive** word. A possessive word tells us who or what something belongs to. For example: in "The dog eats **its** food", the word **its** tells us that the food belongs to the dog.

Write **its** or **it's** in these sentences.

Tomorrow, ... my birthday.

The cup stands on .... saucer.

.... raining again.

The football team changed .... football kit.

Write three sentences of your own using **it's**.

....

....

....

Write three sentences of your own using **its**.

....

....

....

Compound words

FACTS

A **compound word** is formed by joining two short words together to make one new word. For example: **football** is made from **foot** and **ball**.

Make compound words by combining words from the first box with words from the second box and then write them in the empty boxes provided. Start by filling the boxes at the bottom of the page.

For each compound word you make, the ball is kicked closer to the goal. Can you make enough compound words to kick the ball into the goal?

after	foot	back
bed	cloak	to

ball	wards	side
step	noon	room

Bag of compounds

Remember: a **compound word** is made by joining two short words together to make one new word.

Look at the compound words on this bag for one minute.

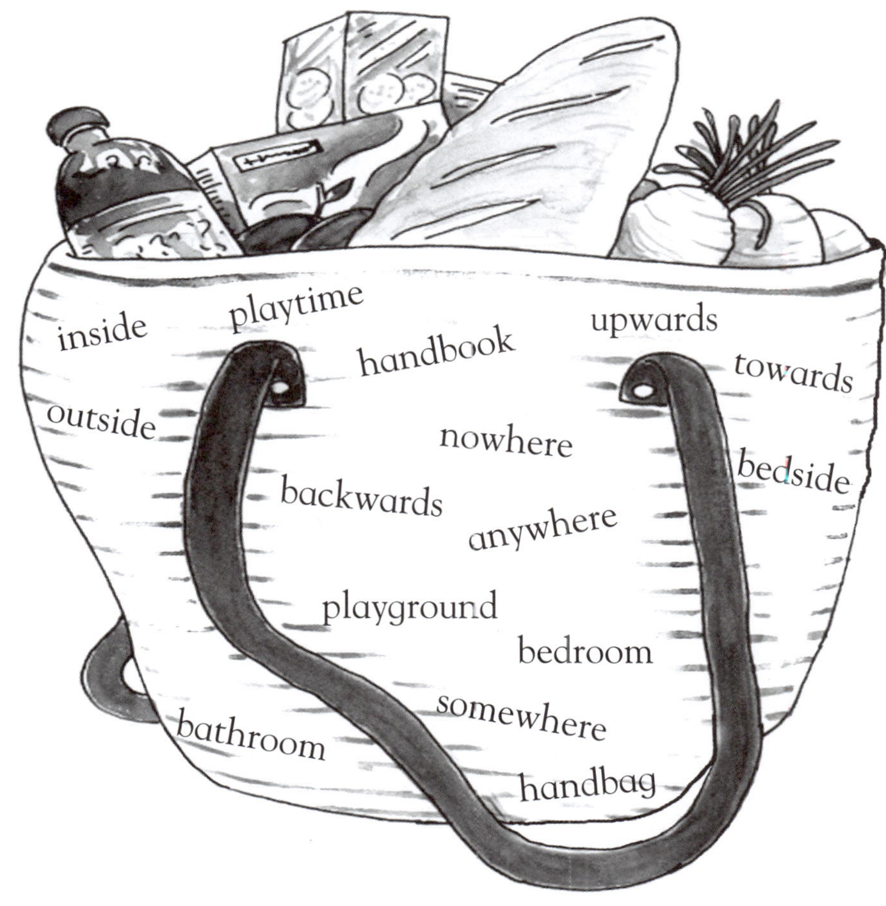

Now cover the bag. How many words can you remember? Complete the missing parts of the words below. The missing parts are all words that make up the compound words on the bag.

play	....................side	....................where
play	....................side	....................where
....................room	hand	....................wards
....................room	hand	....................wards
....................side	....................where	....................wards

Ancient words

FACTS

Words from ancient languages were used to make English words. For example: the Greek words **mikros** and **skopein** mean **small** and **to see**. Together, they make the English word **microscope**, which is an instrument used to **see small** things.

Draw lines from each ancient word below to the modern words that were made from it.

Ancient words	Modern words
graphein — a Greek word meaning **to write**	dictionary
dictare — a Latin word meaning **to say**	telephone
tele — a Greek word meaning **afar**	dictate
aqua — a Latin word meaning **water**	paragraph
	contradict
	aquatic
	telescope
	geography
	aqueduct
	graphs
	photograph
	prediction
	television
	aquarium

Root meanings ★

FACTS

Words from ancient languages often became the **root words** of modern English words. One way of remembering the spelling of a word is to know the **meaning** of its root word.

For each of the following modern words, write a definition that shows you understand the meaning of its root word. Use a dictionary to help you.

Root word = **graph**

photograph ....

paragraph ....

graphs ....

geography ....

Root word = **dict**

prediction ....

dictate ....

dictionary ....

contradiction ....

Spellings to learn

it's afterwards outside playtime somewhere photograph

Spelling practice

FACTS

Writing out words is the best way to learn their spellings.

Look at the four words in each group. Now cover the words and write them in the second column. Then check your spellings and write the words again in the next column. Repeat the exercise using the third and fourth columns.

enough ....
famous ....
suppose ....
popular ....

pressure ....
increase ....
length ....
medicine ....

experiment ....
opposite ....
particular ....
ordinary ....

favourite ....
height ....
important ....
material ....

experience ....
interest ....
natural ....
occasion ....

Answer section with parents' notes

Key Stage 2
Ages 8–9

This eight-page section provides answers and explanatory notes to all the activities in this book, enabling you to assess your child's work.

Work through each page together and ensure that your child understands each task. Point out any mistakes your child makes and correct any errors in spelling. (Your child should use the handwriting style taught at his or her school.) As well as making corrections, it is very important to praise your child's efforts and achievements.

At the end of this section, there is a glossary that includes all the key terms covered in this book.

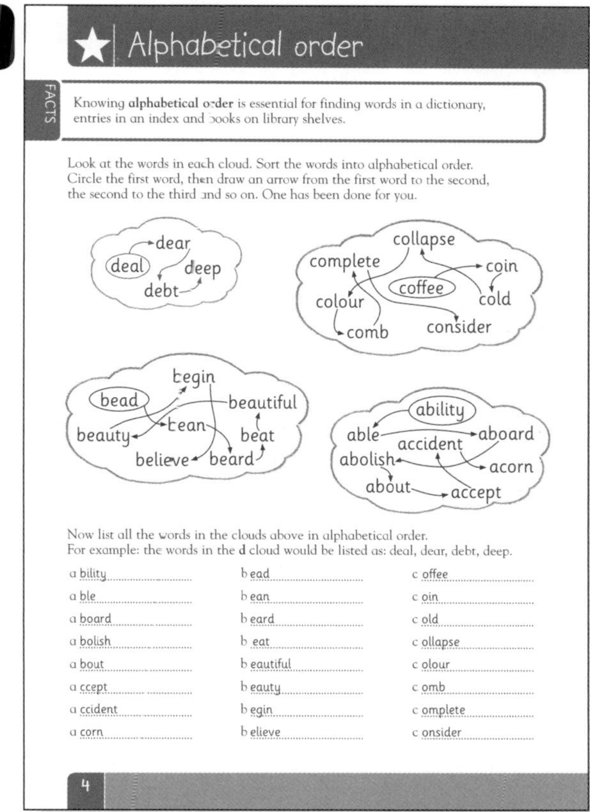

4

Alphabetical order

FACTS

Knowing **alphabetical order** is essential for finding words in a dictionary, entries in an index and books on library shelves.

Look at the words in each cloud. Sort the words into alphabetical order. Circle the first word, then draw an arrow from the first word to the second, the second to the third and so on. One has been done for you.

Now list all the words in the clouds above in alphabetical order.
For example: the words in the **d** cloud would be listed as: deal, dear, debt, deep.

a bility	b ead	c offee
a ble	b ean	c oin
a board	b eard	c old
a bolish	b eat	c ollapse
a bout	b eautiful	c olour
a ccept	b eauty	c omb
a ccident	b egin	c omplete
a corn	b elieve	c onsider

Your chi_ld needs to order the words by comparing the letters of each word. Once he or she has completed this activity, you could check the word order with your child using a dictionary.

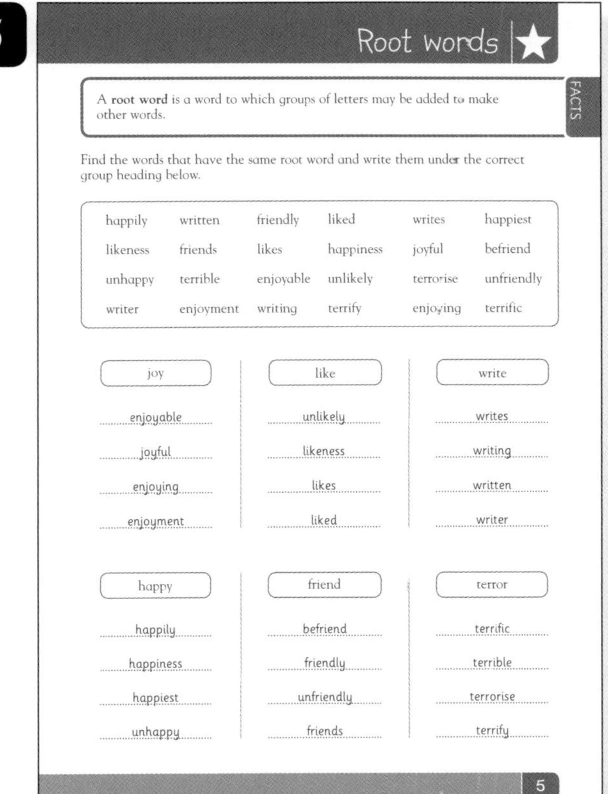

5

Root words

FACTS

A **root word** is a word to which groups of letters may be added to make other words.

Find the words that have the same root word and write them under the correct group heading below.

happily	written	friendly	liked	writes	happiest
likeness	friends	likes	happiness	joyful	befriend
unhappy	terrible	enjoyable	unlikely	terrorise	unfriendly
writer	enjoyment	writing	terrify	enjoying	terrific

joy	like	write
enjoyable	unlikely	writes
joyful	likeness	writing
enjoying	likes	written
enjoyment	liked	writer

happy	friend	terror
happily	befriend	terrific
happiness	friendly	terrible
happiest	unfriendly	terrorise
unhappy	friends	terrify

Words with similar meanings contain similar spelling patterns. As your child does this activity, you could discuss the meanings and identify the similarities with him or her.

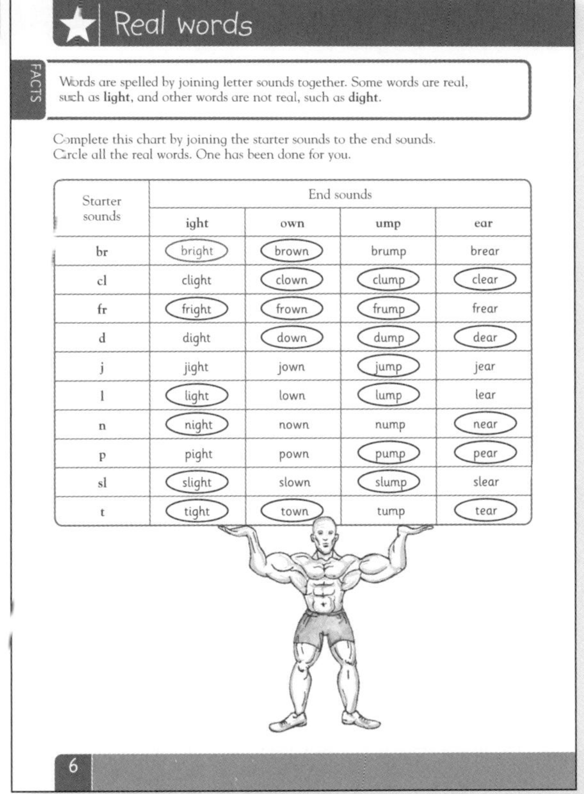

6

Real words

FACTS

Words are spelled by joining letter sounds together. Some words are real, such as **light**, and other words are not real, such as **dight**.

Complete this chart by joining the starter sounds to the end sounds. Circle all the real words. One has been done for you.

Starter sounds	End sounds			
	ight	own	ump	ear
br	bright	brown	brump	brear
cl	clight	clown	clump	clear
fr	fright	frown	frump	frear
d	dight	down	dump	dear
j	jight	jown	jump	jear
l	light	lown	lump	lear
n	night	nown	nump	near
p	pight	pown	pump	pear
sl	slight	slown	slump	slear
t	tight	town	tump	tear

Reading and spelling abilities are developed by applying what is known about the sound and spelling of one word to other words. Ask your child to make sentences using the real words that are made.

7

Homophones

FACTS

Homophones are words that sound the same but have different spellings and meanings. For example:

hole and whole | wait and weight

Look at the homophone pairs in the balloons. Complete these sentences using these words.

We played with our friends.

We played outside for an hour.

We can see the beach.

I played in the sea.

Write four sentences using the homophones in the balloons below.

Answers may vary

Can you think of some more homophone pairs?

Answers may vary

Homophones can cause confusion. Before your child writes the sentences, read and say the words with him or her. You can make notes on the page, distinguishing one spelling from another.

8

Common homophones

FACTS

The word **homophone** comes from the Greek words for **same** and **sound**.

Here are three pairs of common homophones.

Homophones	Meanings	Examples
their	shows something is owned	Their shoes belonged to them.
there	points to a place	The shop is over there.
to	towards a place or person	Give the bag to him.
too	also or as well	I went shopping and Claire came, too.
see	to look at something	I can see you.
sea	a vast amount of salt water	The boat sails on the sea.

Write six sentences using the homophones above.

Answers may vary

Spellings to learn

our hour rain reign new knew heard herd to too

These words are worth learning as a set. After doing the activity, encourage your child to look out for them. They are common words, but they are easily and often confused.

9

Rhyming words

FACTS

Words with the same endings often **rhyme**, as in **right** and **fight**.

Read the words in the book below. Find the seven pairs of rhyming words and write them on the lines. Time yourself. How long does it take you to match and write all the rhyming pairs?

rough dear learn proud weary bear round sound earn wear loud dreary fear tough

dreary	weary	earn	learn
tough	rough	fear	dear
proud	loud	bear	wear
sound	round		

Pairs found in Answers may vary seconds.

Now find seven groups of three rhyming words on this list. Time yourself.

nice	mice	ice
sight	light	bright
should	could	would
applause	cause	pause
your	pour	four
sigh	high	thigh
weight	eight	freight

sight applause ice should nice pause thigh your high pour would bright eight cause sigh mice freight weight four light could

Groups found in Answers may vary seconds.

Similar looking strings of letters can make completely different sounds. Check your child is matching words by their sound and not by how they look. You could read the words together.

10

Verb endings

FACTS

A **verb** is a doing, or action, word. It tells us what happens in a sentence. It can have different endings.

The endings tell us if the action happened in the **past** (for example: **she played**) or if the action happens in the **present** (for example: **she plays** or **she is playing**).

Make three new words from each root verb by adding the different endings. One has been done for you.

Root verbs	Add s	Add ed	Add ing
shout	shouts	shouted	shouting
look	looks	looked	looking
climb	climbs	climbed	climbing
kick	kicks	kicked	kicking
learn	learns	learned	learning
cook	cooks	cooked	cooking
wait	waits	waited	waiting
laugh	laughs	laughed	laughing
clean	cleans	cleaned	cleaning

The three endings **s**, **ed** and **ing** are the basis for spelling different forms of verbs. You can extend the activity by asking your child to make sentences using the three different forms.

11

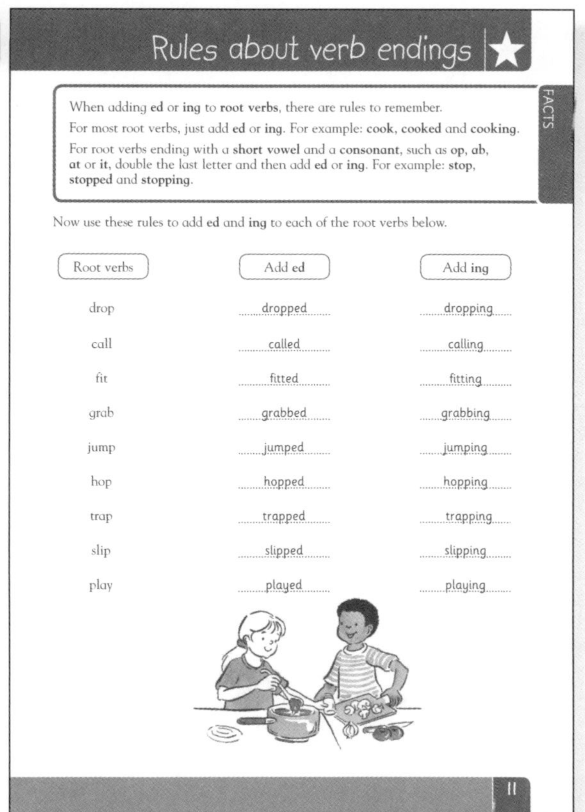

Rules about verb endings

FACTS

When adding **ed** or **ing** to **root verbs**, there are rules to remember.

For most root verbs, just add **ed** or **ing**. For example: **cook, cooked** and **cooking**.

For root verbs ending with a **short vowel** and a **consonant**, such as **op, ab, at** or **it**, double the last letter and then add **ed** or **ing**. For example: **stop, stopped** and **stopping**.

Now use these rules to add **ed** and **ing** to each of the root verbs below.

Root verbs	Add ed	Add ing
drop	dropped	dropping
call	called	calling
fit	fitted	fitting
grab	grabbed	grabbing
jump	jumped	jumping
hop	hopped	hopping
trap	trapped	trapping
slip	slipped	slipping
play	played	playing

11

Words ending in a short vowel and a consonant make confusing exceptions to spelling rules. Saying the vowels in their short sound form, such as **o** in sh**o**p and **i** in p**i**t, makes **a**, **e**, **i**, **o** and **u** sound different.

12

More rules about verb endings

FACTS

Verbs can be changed by adding **ed** and **ing**. When verbs that end in **y** or **e** are changed, there are a couple of rules to remember.

For a **root verb** ending in **e**, drop the **e** before adding the ending.

For a root verb ending in a **consonant** and **y**, change the **y** to **i** before adding **ed**, but keep the **y** before adding **ing**.

Add **ed** and **ing** to each of the root verbs below. One has been done for you.

Root verbs	Add ed	Add ing
hate	hated	hating
change	changed	changing
wave	waved	waving
skate	skated	skating
fade	faded	fading
move	moved	moving

Add **ed** and **ing** to each of the root verbs below. One has been done for you.

Root verbs	Add ed	Add ing
marry	married	marrying
try	tried	trying
cry	cried	crying
deny	denied	denying
rely	relied	relying
carry	carried	carrying

12

This activity will help your child sense words that appear to look right. Experienced spellers see something wrong in spelling **criing** for **crying**, which is why we often write words down to check the spellings.

13

More rules about verb endings

FACTS

Verbs can be changed by adding **s** or **es**, but there are some rules to remember.

For most verbs, just add **s**. For example: **I add** and **she adds**.

For a verb ending in a **consonant** and **y**, change the **y** to **i** and then add **es**. For example: **I worry** and **she worries**.

For a verb ending in a soft sound, such as **ss**, **sh**, **ch** and **x**, add **es**. For example: **I fix** and **she fixes**.

Use the rules above to change the following root verbs.

I look →	She	looks	I wish →	Carla	wishes
I find →	He	finds	I catch →	It	catches
I play →	Liam	plays	I cry →	He	cries
I envy →	She	envies	I make →	It	makes
I help →	He	helps	I try →	She	tries
I pass →	Jo	passes	I change →	It	changes
I run →	He	runs	I carry →	Carol	carries
I rush →	She	rushes	I push →	He	pushes
I want →	He	wants	I fall →	She	falls

13

There is a similarity between the rules here and the rules for plurals. In both cases, the addition of **s** sometimes has to be modified to avoid unpronounceable words like **pushs** and **catchs**.

14

Roots and verbs

FACTS

Remember: a **verb** is a doing, or action, word.

Read the following verbs and find groups of three words with the same root verb. One has been done for you.
Hint: look for three verbs that start with the same letters.

make writing making made keeping taking take kept see catch know wrote keep took knew write seeing saw caught knowing catching

know, knew, knowing	see, saw, seeing
catch, caught, catching	take, took, taking
make, made, making	write, wrote, writing
keep, kept, keeping	

14

Some of the verb endings here do not follow the rules on the previous page. Encourage your child to use the verbs in sentences. He or she needs to learn the irregular spellings and their uses.

15

Irregular verbs ★

FACTS

Not all verbs follow regular verb rules. For example: the past form of **run** is not **runned** but **ran**. We call these **irregular verbs**.

Sort the irregular verbs in the verb box into their present and past forms. One has been done for you.

give can found told see take had am knew make took went go eat know tell ate made could was saw gave have find

Present	Past
see	saw
give	gave
can	could
go	went
tell	told
am	was
take	took
have	had
know	knew
eat	ate
make	made
find	found

15

One way for your child to work out if a verb is in the past or present tense form is to imagine saying the verb after the phrase "Today I..." or "Yesterday I...".

16

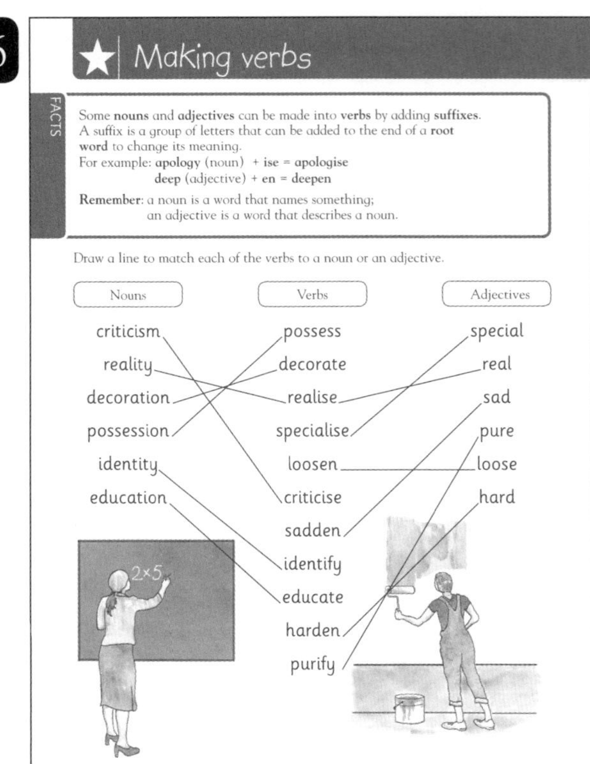

★ Making verbs

FACTS

Some **nouns** and **adjectives** can be made into **verbs** by adding **suffixes**. A suffix is a group of letters that can be added to the end of a **root word** to change its meaning.
For example: **apology** (noun) + **ise** = **apologise**
deep (adjective) + **en** = **deepen**

Remember: a noun is a word that names something; an adjective is a word that describes a noun.

Draw a line to match each of the verbs to a noun or an adjective.

Nouns	Verbs	Adjectives
criticism	possess	special
reality	decorate	real
decoration	realise	sad
possession	specialise	pure
identity	loosen	loose
education	criticise	hard
	sadden	
	identify	
	educate	
	harden	
	purify	

16

This activity shows the connections between grammar and spelling. By adding a suffix, a word can change from one part of speech to another, as shown in the noun-to-verb and verb-to-adjective connections.

17

The prefix "al" ★

FACTS

A **prefix** is a group of letters that can be added to the beginning of a root word to change its meaning. The prefix **al** means **all**.

Add the prefix **al** to each of these root words and then write sentences in the speech bubbles using the new words.

al words

a l so a l ways a l most
a l though a l one a l ready

Answers may vary

17

The prefix **al** means **all**, but it is important to ensure your child uses one **l**. It is very tempting to use **all** at the start of **altogether**, for example. Stress that the prefix just has the one **l**.

18

★ Adding prefixes

FACTS

Remember: a **prefix** changes the meaning of a root word.

Each of the words below has a prefix: **ad**, **al**, **af** or **a**. Write each word in its correct prefix group.

advice adjective asleep already also ahead alike affect almost away affirm always affix adverb admire afflict

ad al af a

ad words	**al** words
advice	already
adjective	also
adverb	almost
admire	always

af words	**a** words
affect	alike
affirm	asleep
affix	ahead
afflict	away

Look in a dictionary for two more words in each prefix group. Add them to the correct list. Now learn the spellings of the words in each group.

18

The prefixes **ad** and **af** mean **to** and the prefix **a** means **on** or **in**. Encourage your child to continue grouping words that begin with the same prefixes, as this awareness may help in remembering spellings.

19

Word bluff

The suffixes **ship, hood, ness** and **ment** are called **state suffixes**. They are used to change root words into new words that describe the state of being something.

member + ship = membership (the state of being a member)

mother + hood = motherhood (the state of being a mother)

Each box below contains a definition and two words. One of the two words is correct and the other is made up. Circle the correct word.

the state of being a knight	the state of being a friend
knightship (knighthood)	friendhood (friendship)
the state of being a champion	the state of being punished
(championship) championhood	(punishment) punishship
the state of enjoying something	the state of being dark
enjoyness (enjoyment)	(darkness) darkment
the state of owning something	the state of being amused
ownerment (ownership)	(amusement) amusehood
the state of being astonished	the state of being ill
(astonishment) astonishhood	(illness) illship
the state of being fit	the state of being a child
(fitness) fitment	(childhood) childship

19

Extend this activity by asking your child to list any words he or she knows that end in the suffixes **ship, hood, ness** and **ment**. Then look at their state-of-being meanings together.

20

The "ight" and "tion" endings

Two common word endings are **ight** and **tion**.

How many words can you make by joining the endings **ight** or **tion** to each of the beginnings below? List the words in the numbered spaces. Can you fill all the spaces?

Beginnings	
br	sta
ac	ton
decora	men
na	n
stra	rela
fr	fre
del	posi

1 bright
2 action
3 decoration
4 nation
5 straight
6 fright
7 delight
8 station
9 tonight
10 mention
11 night
12 relation
13 freight
14 position

I scored Answers may vary points.

20

The best way for your child to do this activity is to try each beginning with both of the **ight** and **tion** endings. He or she can then discard unreal words, such as **menight**, but use the real words, such as **mention**.

21

Root roads

Remember: there is only one **l** in the suffix **ful**.

Start at a root word (on the left) and drive to a suffix (on the right) that will make a new word. Write the new word on a dotted line.

Root words: fashion, arm, self, wise, kind, friend, reason, child, suit, care

Suffixes: ly, ish, able, ful

ly: wisely, kindly, friendly

ish: selfish, childish

able: fashionable, reasonable, suitable

ful: armful, careful

21

Encourage your child to go through a process of elimination. By taking a root word such as **fashion**, and adding each of the suffixes, he or she will find the one that works.

22

Suffix maze

Remember: the final **e** in some words is dropped before the suffix **ive** is added, as in **expense + ive = expensive**.

On the maze, draw a line joining each root word on the left to a suffix on the right to make one of the words in the box below.

helpful	expensive	gladly
artist	careful	active

Root words: expense, act, care, help, glad, art

Suffixes: ive, ful, ist, ly

Spellings to learn

recent action tonight lovely careful friendly

22

Here, your child is introduced to the suffixes **ive** and **ist**, and revisits the suffixes **ful** and **ly**. Ask your child if he or she can think of any other words with these endings.

23

Similar suffixes

FACTS

Some suffixes sound similar, such as **ible** and **able**; **tion** and **sion**.
The suffix **able** usually follows a root word that makes sense on its own.
For example: **agree** makes sense on its own.
The suffix **ible** usually follows a root that is not an actual word.
For example: if you take the **ible** from **horrible**, it leaves **horr**.

Complete the following words using **ible** or **able**. Use a dictionary to check your answers.

terrible	comfortable
reasonable	impossible
sensible	remarkable
suitable	laughable
visible	horrible
possible	agreeable

Complete the following words using **tion** or **sion**. Use a dictionary to check your answers.

division	television
explosion	competition
information	protection
invention	invasion
revision	nation
tension	action
vision	publication

23

The "actual word" rule is a way of differentiating between words with the **ible** and **able** endings. Encourage your child to say each root word aloud and consider whether or not it is a real word.

24

Making plurals

FACTS

For **singular nouns** that end in **f**, **ff** or **fe**, there are three rules to remember when making them **plural**.

If the word ends in a single **f**, you usually change **f** to **v** and add **es**.	If the word ends in **fe**, change **fe** to **ves**.	If the word ends in **ff**, just add **s**.
For example:	For example:	For example:
scarf	**wife**	**cuff**
scarves	**wives**	**cuffs**

Write the plurals for these singular nouns.

one leaf → many leaves

one thief → many thieves

one cliff → many cliffs

one loaf → many loaves

one shelf → many shelves

one sniff → many sniffs

24

The **v** plurals are often misspelled, but remembering the rules helps your child distinguish them. Having tried the words here, he or she could try making plurals of other words ending with **ff** or **fe**.

25

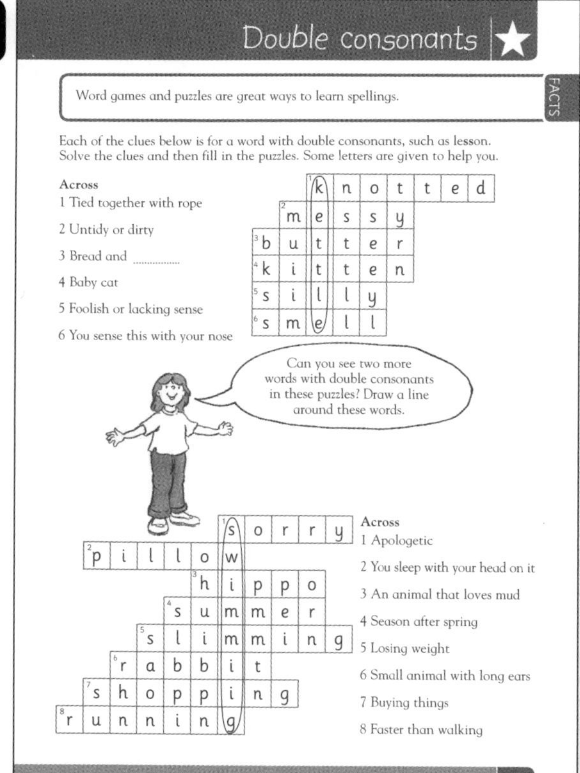

Double consonants

FACTS

Word games and puzzles are great ways to learn spellings.

Each of the clues below is for a word with double consonants, such as lesson. Solve the clues and then fill in the puzzles. Some letters are given to help you.

Across
1 Tied together with rope
2 Untidy or dirty
3 Bread and ....
4 Baby cat
5 Foolish or lacking sense
6 You sense this with your nose

1 knotted
2 messy
3 butter
4 kitten
5 silly
6 smell

Across
1 Apologetic
2 You sleep with your head on it
3 An animal that loves mud
4 Season after spring
5 Losing weight
6 Small animal with long ears
7 Buying things
8 Faster than walking

1 sorry
2 pillow
3 hippo
4 summer
5 slimming
6 rabbit
7 shopping
8 running

25

Using a double letter in a word can be easily missed because the sound is the same as for a single letter. When solving each clue, your child needs to think about which letter in the word is doubled.

26

Strings and sounds

FACTS

Some **letter strings** make different sounds when they are used in different words.
For example: the letters **oo** sound different in book and hoot.

Look at the words in the word box. Write the words with the same letter strings in the correct letter string list.

tool	screw	foot	blood	mission	chemist
loose	work	chop	bench	ascend	session
worn	waste	swam	punch	lesson	scrape
miss	was	swan	worth	sword	science

ch	oo	sc
bench	tool	science
punch	blood	scrape
chop	foot	screw
chemist	loose	ascend

wa	ss	wor
swan	lesson	sword
swam	session	worn
waste	mission	worth
was	miss	work

Spellings to learn

daring swimming playful beautiful reasonable television

26

As your child separates certain words and allocates them to certain letter strings, encourage him or her to look at the different ways in which those strings are pronounced.

27

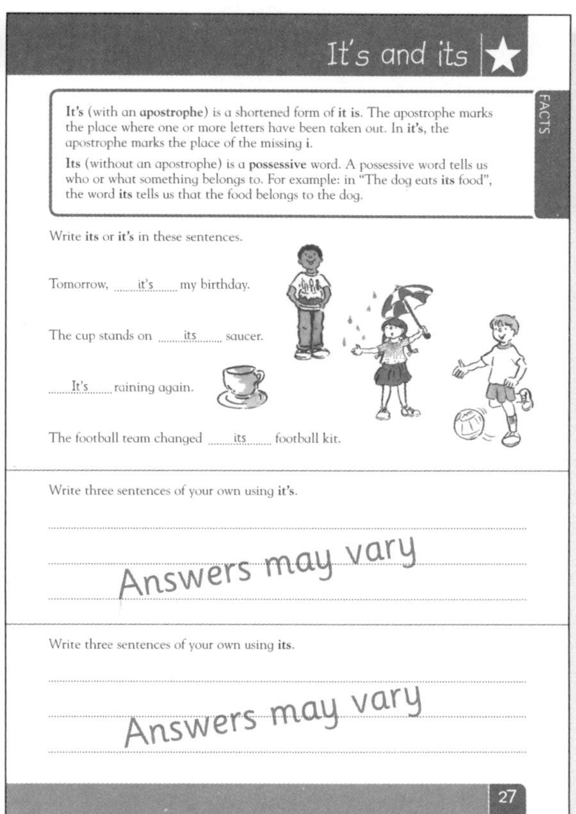

It's and its

FACTS

It's (with an **apostrophe**) is a shortened form of **it is**. The apostrophe marks the place where one or more letters have been taken out. In **it's**, the apostrophe marks the place of the missing **i**.

Its (without an apostrophe) is a **possessive** word. A possessive word tells us who or what something belongs to. For example: in "The dog eats **its** food", the word **its** tells us that the food belongs to the dog.

Write **its** or **it's** in these sentences.

Tomorrow, it's my birthday.

The cup stands on its saucer.

It's raining again.

The football team changed its football kit.

Write three sentences of your own using **it's**.

Answers may vary

Write three sentences of your own using **its**.

Answers may vary

27

Understanding the use of the apostrophe is the key to this activity. Encourage your child to read the information, which will help him or her distinguish between **it's** and **its**.

28

Compound words

FACTS

A **compound word** is formed by joining two short words together to make one new word. For example: **football** is made from **foot** and **ball**.

Make compound words by combining words from the first box with words from the second box and then write them in the empty boxes provided. Start by filling the boxes at the bottom of the page.

For each compound word you make, the ball is kicked closer to the goal. Can you make enough compound words to kick the ball into the goal?

after foot back
bed cloak to

ball wards side
step noon room

towards
backside
backwards
bedroom
bedside
footstep
football
afterwards
afternoon
cloakroom

28

To extend this activity, encourage your child to look for other compound words in the dictionary. Can he or she find other words that begin or end with the words given in this activity?

29

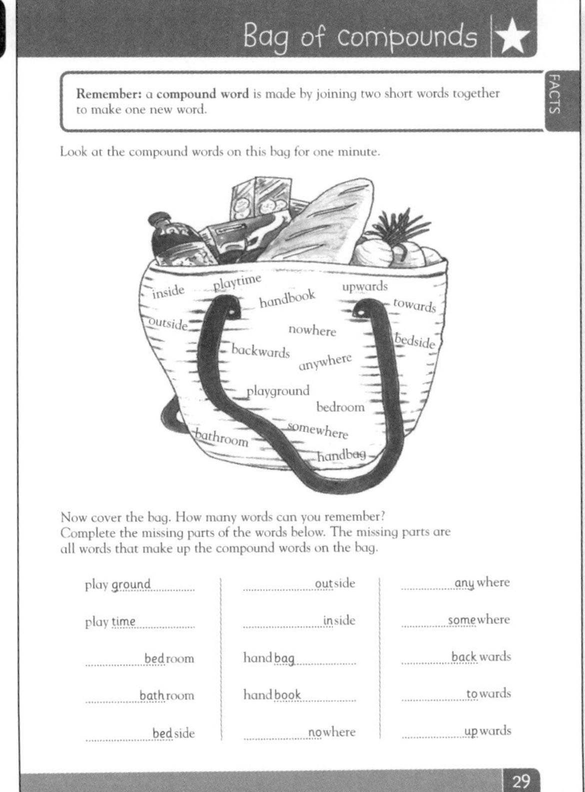

Bag of compounds

FACTS

Remember: a **compound word** is made by joining two short words together to make one new word.

Look at the compound words on this bag for one minute.

Now cover the bag. How many words can you remember? Complete the missing parts of the words below. The missing parts are all words that make up the compound words on the bag.

play ground	out side	any where
play time	in side	some where
bed room	hand bag	back wards
bath room	hand book	to wards
bed side	no where	up wards

29

Your child needs to make connections between the words on the bag, such as **handbook** and **handbag**, which both start with **hand**. If necessary, allow your child another look at the bag.

30

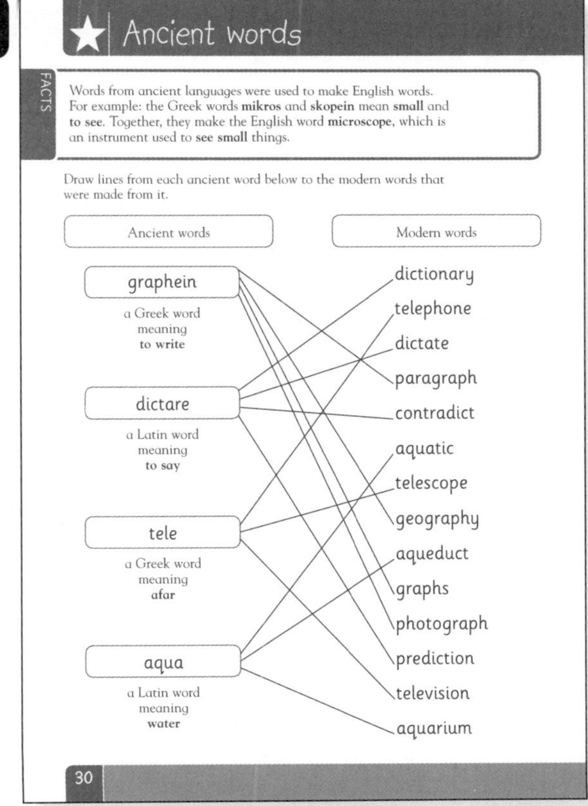

Ancient words

FACTS

Words from ancient languages were used to make English words. For example: the Greek words **mikros** and **skopein** mean **small** and **to see**. Together, they make the English word **microscope**, which is an instrument used to **see small** things.

Draw lines from each ancient word below to the modern words that were made from it.

Ancient words	Modern words
graphein a Greek word meaning **to write**	dictionary
	telephone
	dictate
dictare a Latin word meaning **to say**	paragraph
	contradict
	aquatic
tele a Greek word meaning **afar**	telescope
	geography
	aqueduct
aqua a Latin word meaning **water**	graphs
	photograph
	prediction
	television
	aquarium

30

The meaning of many modern words can be worked out from understanding their roots, such as **aqua** in **aquarium**. Familiarity with common roots will help your child notice them in other words.

31

Root meanings ★

FACTS

Words from ancient languages often became the **root words** of modern English words. One way of remembering the spelling of a word is to know the **meaning** of its root word.

For each of the following modern words, write a definition that shows you understand the meaning of its root word. Use a dictionary to help you.

Root word = **graph**

photograph	This is like writing or recording a moment as a picture.
paragraph	This is a number of written lines.
graphs	A way to show numbers in a written form.
geography	Writing about and studying the Earth.

Root word = **dict**

prediction	This is to say something about the future.
dictate	To say words that are then written down.
dictionary	A book that says the meanings of words.
contradiction	To say the opposite to what has been said.

Spellings to learn

it's afterwards outside playtime somewhere photograph

31

Pages 30 and 31 show how English has absorbed words from other languages, such as Latin and Greek. Dictionaries may include etymology (word origins) in their entries. Help your child look up the origins of some words.

32

★ Spelling practice

FACTS

Writing out words is the best way to learn their spellings.

Look at the four words in each group. Now cover the words and write them in the second column. Then check your spellings and write the words again in the next column. Repeat the exercise using the third and fourth columns.

enough	enough	enough	enough	enough
famous	famous	famous	famous	famous
suppose	suppose	suppose	suppose	suppose
popular	popular	popular	popular	popular
pressure	pressure	pressure	pressure	pressure
increase	increase	increase	increase	increase
length	length	length	length	length
medicine	medicine	medicine	medicine	medicine
experiment	experiment	experiment	experiment	experiment
opposite	opposite	opposite	opposite	opposite
particular	particular	particular	particular	particular
ordinary	ordinary	ordinary	ordinary	ordinary
favourite	favourite	favourite	favourite	favourite
height	height	height	height	height
important	important	important	important	important
material	material	material	material	material
experience	experience	experience	experience	experience
interest	interest	interest	interest	interest
natural	natural	natural	natural	natural
occasion	occasion	occasion	occasion	occasion

32

Ask your child to say sentences that include these words to show that he or she understands their meanings. For example: "My trip to London was a great experience" or "We take medicine to get better."

Glossary

Adjective
A describing word, such as **hot**.

Apostrophe
A punctuation mark to replace letters that have been removed, as in **it's**. It is also used to show possession, as in **Jack's pencil**.

Compound words
Two words put together to make one word, such as **playground**.

Contraction
Two words joined together to make one word with an apostrophe for missing letters. Examples include **don't** (do not) and **it's** (it is).

Homophones
Words that sound the same but have different spellings and meanings, such as **sight** and **site**.

Irregular verb
A verb with unusual spelling changes when the tense or subject changes, such as **to be** (he is; they are; we were).

Letter string
A letter sequence in a word that makes a sound. It may have more than one pronunciation, such as **ough** in **cough** and **rough**.

Noun
A word for an object, person, place, quality or state. Examples include: **leaf**, **joy**, **sea** and **mother**.

Past tense
A verb telling us about an action that happened in the past. For example: **Polly laughed**.

Plural
More than one of something. We usually, but not always, add an **s** to the singular. For example: **tigers**.

Possessive word
A word that tells what something belongs to, such as **its** and **her**.

Prefix
A group of letters put before a root word that changes its meaning, such as **de**, **re**, **in**, **un** and **dis**.

Present tense
When a verb tell us about an action happening in the present. For example: **Dylan sees** or **Lucy is dancing**.

Rhyming words
Words ending in a similar sound, such as **book** and **shook**.

Root word
The form of a word without any suffixes or prefixes. For example: **care** is the root word of **careful**.

Singular
One of something, such as a **coin**.

Suffix
A group of letters added to the end of a root word to change its meaning or usage. Examples include **able**, **ive** and **ly**.

Verb
A doing, or action, word, such as (to) **jump**, **cough** and **write**.